T0026461

TO:

FROM:

"I don't care what anyone says. Being rich is a good thing."

—MARK CUBAN

H$W RICH PEOPLE THINK

STEVE SIEBOLD

Photo Credits

Internal images © page 44, 99, 130, Rawpixel.com/Shutterstock; page 76, Flamingo Images/Shutterstock; page 113, everything possible/Shutterstock

All other images have been provided by Pexels, Pixabay, Unsplash, or Wikimedia Commons; these images are licensed under CC0 Creative Commons and have been released by the author for public use.

Published by Simple Truths, an imprint of Sourcebooks

P.O. Box 4410, Naperville, Illinois 60567-4410

(630) 961-3900

sourcebooks.com

Originally published in 2010 in the United States by London House Press. This edition issued based on the hardcover edition published in 2014 in the United States by Simple Truths, an imprint of Sourcebooks.

Printed and bound in China.

OGP 10 9 8 7 6 5 4 3 2

CONTENTS

INTRODUCTION

THIS BOOK ISN'T ABOUT MONEY. It's about *thinking*. Each short chapter represents one of the lessons I've learned over the past twenty-six years interviewing some of the richest people in the world. Every chapter compares the "middle class" and "world class." These terms reference the average person versus the world-class thinker. The idea is to compare the way most people think about money in contrast to the rich. The differences are as extreme as they are numerous.

When I started this journey in 1984, I was a college

student, completely broke and searching for answers about success I wasn't finding in the classroom. My discoveries along the way changed my life, and I wrote this book to give you the same opportunity. If you follow the beliefs, philosophies, and strategies of the rich and take action, you have a legitimate shot at becoming a millionaire. The secret is not in the mechanics of money but in the level of thinking that generates it. Once you learn to embrace this, your earning potential is limitless.

If you find yourself saying "not all rich people

believe this or do that,"—*of course* you're right. I based these comparisons on what the majority of rich people shared with me. This also applies to what I say about the masses.

I interviewed rich people because I wanted to be rich. What I discovered was, to get rich, I had to learn to think like a rich person. I spent the first twenty-five years of my life thinking about money like the masses, which kept me broke. Once I changed my thinking, the money started to flow. The changes began with my thinking, which led me to take effective action that eventually made me a millionaire. Don't be impressed or intimidated by my success or anyone else's, because you can do exactly the same thing. Let this book be your guide.

I wish you the best of luck on your journey. Please let me know how you're progressing by visiting mental-toughnessblog.com and sharing your story.

All the best,

STEVE SIEBOLD

Middle Class Focuses on Savings, World Class Focuses on Earning

DRIVEN BY THE FEAR OF LOSS AND UNCERTAINTY OF THE FUTURE, THE MASSES FOCUS ON HOW TO PROTECT AND HOARD THEIR MONEY. While world-class thinkers understand the importance of saving and investing, they direct their mental energy toward accumulating wealth through serving people and solving problems.

When an economic correction occurs, the fear-based saver suffers catastrophic losses that may take years to recover. While world-class thinkers suffer similar losses, they quickly turn their attention to financial opportunities that present themselves in a society of suddenly terrified people. While the masses are selling for short-term survival, the great ones are buying for long-term success. One group is operating from fear; the other from abundance.

The self-made rich aren't afraid to take calculated risks, because they know if they lose, they can make it all back. While the middle class is always looking for the home-run investment that will make them wealthy, the world class invests wisely, knowing the bulk of their fortune will come from the service they provide. Most people are more concerned with the modest gains they accumulate from their savings and investments than they are with using their billion-dollar minds to create a fortune. The masses are so focused on clipping coupons and living frugally that they miss major opportunities. Even in the midst of a cash-flow crisis, the rich reject the nickel-and-dime thinking of the masses. They are masters at focusing their mental energy where it belongs: on the big money.

How about you? Are you more focused on saving pennies or building an empire? Your current financial status will give you an idea of your past thinking. If you're rich, keep thinking the way you're thinking. If not, maybe it's time for a change.

Rich Resource:

▶ *The Rich: A New Study of the Species* by William Davis

Critical Thinking Question:

▶ Based on your past behaviors and results, are you thinking big or small?

Action Step:

▶ Make a decision today to think bigger and maximize your money potential.

"Money is power, and you ought to be reasonably ambitious to have it."

—RUSSELL CONWELL

Middle Class Thinks about Money in Linear Terms, World Class Thinks about Money in Nonlinear Terms

THE MASSES TRADE TIME FOR MONEY. This creates the belief that making money is a linear process directly connected to time. The average person believes the only way to earn more money is to work more hours, with the exception of raises and bonuses. The wealthy know big money requires thinking about it in nonlinear terms. The great ones are masters at generating money through ideas that solve problems. They realize that since there are no limits to ideas, there is no limit to how much money they can earn. So while the middle class is scrambling to survive and frightened for their financial future, the world class is capitalizing on their elevated level of awareness.

The masses waste a substantial percentage of their mental energy worrying about money, while the champions are fearlessly directing their focus to becoming wealthier every day. Fortunes can be created almost overnight with the right idea at the right time, but only if the performer understands this nonlinear phenomena. Since most people think of making money in a linear fashion, they never invest the necessary effort to create high-impact solutions. The truth is, people who educate themselves in this philosophy have the potential to become as wealthy as they wish. And while this has been proven again and again, the average person's refusal to believe this holds them back from ever getting started. This is another reason on the long list of why the rich get richer and the poor get poorer.

Rich Resource:

▶ *The Intelligent Investor* by Benjamin Graham

Critical Thinking Question:

▶ When you're problem solving, do you spend more time looking for the obvious answer or the nonobvious answer? Linear thinking is the obvious, and nonlinear thinking is the nonobvious.

Action Step:

▶ Always look for the obvious, simple, linear solution first. If that doesn't work, start brainstorming the nonobvious, more complex, nonlinear solutions.

"The entire essence of America is the hope to first make money—then to make money with money— then make lots of money with lots of money."

—PAUL ERDMAN

Middle Class Believes Hard Work Creates Wealth, World Class Believes Leverage Creates Wealth

IF HARD WORK WAS THE SECRET TO FINANCIAL SUCCESS, EVERY CONSTRUCTION WORKER AND COCKTAIL WAITRESS WOULD BE RICH. The wealthy strategically focus their efforts on the most profitable areas of their business while leveraging their contacts, credibility, and resources to maximize the results of every action they take. World-class performers work hard, but not in the traditional sense. Hard work to the wealthy means outthinking their competitors and leveraging the collective brainpower of their advisers. The middle class sees hard work as a badge of honor; the world class sees success as a more important badge of honor. While one group is mentally and physically exhausted at the end of the day, the other is fresh and excited about thinking of new solutions and ideas that will keep the first group employed. As a result, the middle class lives paycheck to paycheck, and the world class lives without limits. The only real difference lies in their approach and ability to use leverage in place of linear effort.

The average person is playing life's proverbial slot machine, while the wealthy own the slot machines. The beauty of living in a capitalistic society is that anyone in the middle class is free to make the necessary changes in thinking to capitalize on the concept. Most people won't do it because they are either unaware of how they can think differently or they don't believe it's possible. Either way, the wealthy will continue to amass fortunes while the masses sit on the sidelines, worrying about how to pay their bills.

Rich Resource:

▶ *Your Money and Your Brain: How the New Science of Neuroeconomics Can Help Make You Rich* by Jason Zweig

Critical Thinking Question:

▶ What were you taught about hard work when you were growing up?

Action Step:

▶ Make a decision to let go of any limiting beliefs you have about hard work, and start thinking about how you can use leverage to become more successful.

"People with leverage have dominance over people with less leverage. In other words, just as humans gained advantages over animals by creating leveraged tools, similarly, humans who use these tools of leverage have more power over humans that do not. Saying it more simply, 'leverage is power.'"

—ROBERT KIYOSAKI

Middle Class Believes Money Is Complicated, World Class Believes Money Is Simple

THE MASSES BELIEVE MAKING MONEY IS MYSTERIOUS. World-class thinkers know money flows from ideas. They know that the more value they create in the marketplace, the wealthier they will become. The great ones are masters at converting critical areas of life to simple formulas anyone can follow. Getting rich in a free-market economy is simply a matter of trading solutions for money. The bigger the solution, the bigger the paycheck. It's that simple. The masses

have always thought rich people are smarter, luckier, or more educated. Of course, none of these things are true. The rich see making money through the eyes of endless possibilities and aren't afraid to stake their claim. No matter how often they fail, they persist until they succeed. Their mindset is rooted in the abundant potential every new idea presents, and they live in a consciousness full of excitement and grand anticipation.

So while the middle class approaches money with the mind of an overanalytical academic, the world class approaches money like a child who doesn't understand limitation and honestly believes he can do anything. One group is satisfied with the statistical improbabilities of getting wealthy and resigns to be happy settling for less, and the other ignores the statistics and conquers the world. Making money may not be easy, but it is simple. There is no mystery to getting rich, but this limiting belief stops most people from ever trying. Has it ever stopped you? Is it stopping you now?

Rich Resource:

▶ *Jim Cramer's Real Money: Sane Investing in an Insane World* by James J. Cramer

Critical Thinking Question:

▶ Do you believe you have what it takes to be rich?

Action Step:

▶ Just for today, keep telling yourself that making money is simple and notice how it makes you feel.

"Successful people make money. It's not that people who make money become successful, but that successful people attract money. They bring success to what they do."

—WAYNE DYER

5

Middle Class Believes Building Wealth Is a Solitary Effort, World Class Believes Building Wealth Is a Team Effort

THE AVERAGE PERSON CLOCKS IN AT NINE AND OUT AT FIVE. They are paid for the results of their individual efforts. This limits what they're worth to an organization. The world class knows it takes a team to build wealth, and they focus much of their effort on finding the right people to leverage their actions and ideas. The greatest fortunes are built through the collective mental and physical contributions of a world-class team. The rich see themselves as team leaders, whether their

teams consist of employees, partners, or outsourced contractors. They assemble their team and carefully orchestrate each move the team makes according to a well-planned strategy. While the masses are interested in getting personal credit for the results they achieve, the great ones happily give the credit to their teams and prefer to trade personal recognition for profit. So as the middle class proudly displays their ribbons, trophies, and gold watches, the world class sees their reward as a growing net worth. One group is content to be comfortable, and the other is content to be rich. And one of the primary differences rests in the rich's willingness and ability to build a team and share the credit. Since the masses don't make much money, they crave recognition. The masses are more ego-focused than results-oriented. The great ones want to win and are more than willing to feed the egos of their teammates in exchange for profits.

Rich Resource:

▶ *The Complete Idiot's Guide to Making Money on Wall Street* by Christy Heady

Critical Thinking Question:

▶ Are you willing to trade recognition for riches?

Action Step:

▶ Select an important project you've been pursuing alone and assemble a team of people to help you.

"Teamwork is so important that it is virtually impossible for you to reach the heights of your capabilities or make the money that you want without becoming very good at it."

—BRIAN TRACY

Middle Class Sees Money through the Eyes of Emotion, World Class Sees Money through the Eyes of Logic

MOST PEOPLE NEVER ACCUMULATE MUCH MONEY DUE TO A SERIES OF SELF-LIMITING BELIEFS FUELED BY NEGATIVE EMOTION. By the time the average person becomes an adult, he or she has been brainwashed with dozens of middle-class beliefs and philosophies about money that virtually guarantee a life of financial mediocrity. Children, teenagers, and young adults hear negative money messages over and over until they become beliefs that dictate their behavior. Their well-meaning village of advisers has inadvertently set them up to struggle for the rest of their lives. In short: a middle-class thinker can't teach you how to become a world-class thinker. Someone living a restricted existence can't tell you how to live an unrestricted existence, and a poor person can't teach you how to get rich. These statements are obvious to any rational-thinking person operating from a logic-based mindset.

Few people are able to think about money without clouding the subject with negative emotion, which is generated from dozens of middle-class beliefs. An ordinarily smart, well-educated, and otherwise successful person can be instantly transformed into a fear-based, scarcity-driven thinker whose greatest financial aspiration is to retire comfortably. The world class sees money for what it is and what it's not through the eyes of logic. The great ones know money is a critical tool that presents options and opportunities. They also know if you're not happy without it, you won't be happy with it. But while money has little to do with happiness, it's one of the most important tools in the game of life, and without the psychological chains binding them, champions earn all they can. When it comes to thinking about money, put your emotions on the shelf and let reason be your guide.

Rich Resource:

▶ *How I Raised Myself from Failure to Success in Selling* by Frank Bettger

Critical Thinking Question:

▶ Is your approach to wealth-building based more on logic or emotion?

Action Step:

▶ Decide today to use logic to dictate your financial strategy and emotion to motivate yourself to stick to it.

"A wise man should have money in his head, but not in his heart."

—JONATHAN SWIFT

7

Middle Class Believes Money Is about Status, World Class Believes Money Is about Freedom

AMONG THE MANY MONEY ISSUES MISPERCEIVED BY THE GENERAL PUBLIC IS THE NOTION THAT ACQUIRING GREAT WEALTH IS MORE ABOUT SHOWING OFF THAN CREATING CHOICES. While money certainly brings status, it's acquired mostly for the purpose of attaining personal liberty. It's impossible to be truly free without wealth. The middle class is controlled by employers, government, and other entities with superior resources who dictate what they can and can't do. It's tough to make a moral stand for freedom when you're worried about making your next mortgage payment. Rich people can afford to stand up and fight oppression. They can afford to buy their way out of unhealthy work environments, bad bosses, and other unpleasant situations. They have the means to enlist the best doctors when they get sick and are able to make themselves as comfortable as possible when they can't get well. When they want to voice their opinions, they call their congressman, who wouldn't even consider not returning their call. When the rich want to raise money for business, politics, or charity, a few phone calls to their rich friends is all it takes. If they need more money, they throw a party or host an auction and charge $1,000 a ticket.

The examples of how money buys freedom are endless. The middle class and the world class might live in the same world, but they do not share the same level of freedom. While this infuriates the masses, it motivates the ambitious to get rich. I'm not saying this is right or the way society should be; I'm saying this is the way it is. Instead of wasting your mental energy getting mad, direct it toward getting rich.

Rich Resource:

▶ *The Perfect Portfolio: A Revolutionary Approach to Personal Investing* by Leland B. Hevner

Critical Thinking Question:

▶ Do you believe being rich will increase your level of freedom?

Action Step:

▶ Make a list of the freedoms you will gain when you are wealthy.

"The only thing that money gives you is the freedom of not worrying about money."

—JOHNNY CARSON

8

Middle Class Believes the More Money You Earn, the More Stress You Experience, World Class Believes the More Money You Earn, the Less Stress You Experience

THE AVERAGE PERSON BELIEVES HIGH INCOME EQUALS HIGH STRESS. Successful, high-energy, goal-driven people are often seen as fast-moving and hard-driving, which makes them appear as though they are living a stressful existence. College students are often advised to focus their studies on a field that will allow them to earn a respectable salary while still being able to enjoy their lives, implying that making big money will make them miserable. The world class believes the more money you make, the less stress you will have, because most problems can be solved by writing a check.

Most stress created in business and in relationships is caused by a lack of money, so the more financial resources you have, the less stress you will experience. The rich often make the point that if you want to eliminate stress and spend more time with your family, the most expeditious path is to get rich enough to quit your job. Many corporate employees earning six-figure salaries and a bevy of bonuses are actually part of the working-class poor because they spend more than they make, all the while worrying about not having sufficient time with their family. These otherwise intelligent people rarely realize that with a few adjustments in their belief systems and behaviors, they could earn more money in a week than they currently earn in a year.

The belief that blocks them is they think the only way to earn more money is through more hours, harder work, or promotion. They believe money is made in a linear fashion, which limits what they can earn. The people who embrace nonlinear approaches to building wealth have the world at their fingertips. They are in control of how much they earn and how much stress they expose themselves to. The secret to ascending to this level is realizing that it will take a different set of beliefs and philosophies to make it happen.

Rich Resource:

▶ *The Pocket Idiot's Guide to Investing in Stocks* by Theresa Hamacher CFA, Randy Burgess, and Carl Baldassarre

Critical Thinking Question:

▶ Do you believe getting rich will reduce the level of stress you experience?

Action Step:

▶ Imagine the additional mental energy you would have available to dedicate to your dream without the stress of worrying about money.

"Money is only used for two things. One, it's to make you comfortable, and the more comfortable you are, the more creative you will become. And the other purpose is it enables you to extend the service you provide far beyond your own presence."

—BOB PROCTOR

Middle Class Believes It's Shrewd to Be Cynical, World Class Believes It's Shrewd to Be Optimistic

THE MAJORITY OF THE POPULATION OPERATES FROM FEAR-BASED THINKING AND EMBRACES THE LIMITING BELIEF THAT CYNICISM IS THEIR SAFEST BET. After all, their fear tells them, "If I don't expect much, I won't be disappointed." World-class thinkers rise to riches through an optimistic approach to business and life. They believe everything they touch will turn to gold, and when it doesn't, they believe their next idea will. Optimism is the psychological insulator that keeps them moving forward, no matter how often they fail. Make no mistake: the great ones fail. As a matter of fact, they fail so often that you might label them "professional failures." The difference is when the masses fail, they get depressed and often never attempt anything substantial again. When millionaires fail, they shrug it off and move on to their next idea. They understand what failure is, but to them, it looks like a stepping stone to their next success. And because they don't experience the same psychological pain as the masses when they fail, they keep trying new ideas until they strike gold. Their true power rests in their optimism. They have the courage to bypass their ego and get up when they get knocked down. In the early stages, before they are rich, their failures earn them jeers and snide remarks from friends, family, and others who see them as foolhardy. When they eventually break through and build their fortunes, these same people call them lucky.

While the skeptics search for new ways to explain the shocking success of their friends or relatives, the rich are already on to their next project that promises to make them even wealthier. They've learned to ignore critics who sit on the sidelines and scorn their success, all the while being optimistic that someday they will see the light.

Rich Resource:

▶ *Financial Basics: A Money-Management Guide for Students* by Susan Knox

Critical Thinking Question:

▶ On a scale of one to seven, seven being most optimistic, how optimistic are you? If you scored less than seven, how much is it costing you?

Action Step:

▶ Make a decision today to become a world-class optimist.

"Pessimism leads to weakness, optimism to power."

—WILLIAM JAMES

10

Middle Class Believes Money Is Negative, World Class Believes Money Is Positive

ASK MOST PEOPLE ABOUT MONEY AND YOU'LL UNDERSTAND WHY THEY DON'T HAVE ANY. The masses see ambitious people as greedy and self-serving. They see money as a necessary evil that must be managed but never focused on. After all, there are more righteous pursuits, like television, sports, and movies. The idea of building wealth seems shallow. It also seems like a lot of work.

The rich see money as a positive tool with the power

to create freedom and opportunity for themselves and their families. Being wealthy gives them the option to live what author/philosopher Ayn Rand called "an unrestricted existence." This means having the ability to do what they want, when they want, with whomever they want, for as long as they want, without limitations. It also gives them the freedom to engage in their favorite pastimes, no matter how lavish or seemingly impractical to the masses. Many millionaires form charitable foundations and donate substantial sums to the less fortunate. Without the ongoing support of wealthy benefactors, most charities would not survive.

So while the middle class demonizes and criticizes the world class for selfishness and greed, the latter is donating a lion's share of the money that keeps charities alive. Many also pay more taxes in a year than most people pay in a lifetime and are essentially responsible for funding the infrastructure of the government's tax base. At the heart of this level of thinking is the belief that money is either a tool of evil or empowerment.

The belief you adopt will lead you to abundant wealth or middle-class mediocrity.

Rich Resource:

▶ *I Can Make You Rich* by Paul McKenna

Critical Thinking Question:

▶ Do you believe being rich creates more opportunities or more problems?

Action Step:

▶ Make a list of the things you would do if you were a millionaire.

"A man with a surplus can control circumstances, but a man without a surplus is controlled by them, and often he has no opportunity to exercise judgment."

—HARVEY S. FIRESTONE

11

Middle Class Embraces Advanced Degrees, World Class Embraces Any Form of Education That Makes Them Wealthier

THE MASSES BELIEVE FORMAL EDUCATION IS THE ONLY EDUCATION THAT WILL HELP THEM BECOME SUCCESSFUL. When they want to make more money, their companies encourage them to go back to school and get an MBA or PhD. Employers are often willing to pay for these advanced degrees. This is one of the most inefficient strategies for increasing your income. The most efficient and profitable way is to solve a problem no one else can solve—and sell it. The bigger the problem, the bigger the compensation. This is the cornerstone of every great fortune. Sometimes it takes more education, and that's when world-class thinkers turn to any form of education that will give them the knowledge they need to get what they want. Sometimes they find it in a college classroom, but more often they turn to people who have done what they want to do. This is why personal and professional development seminars have become so popular over the years. Speakers, authors, and trainers who lead these programs have usually achieved massive success in their chosen field and have come back to share their secrets with others who wish to do the same. Some aspiring rich people join referral marketing or direct sales organizations to make money while getting a world-class education in entrepreneurship. This is another unconventional yet extremely effective method of learning from brilliant rich people who have amassed personal fortunes.

The rich and ambitious are also great fans of self-study through the use of books, audio programs,

and other educational materials. They will educate themselves by interviewing successful people in their field. They will hire personal coaches and consultants. They will tap any form of education available to make their dreams a reality, and they don't need a diploma or certificate of completion to validate their investment. So, while the middle class tends to limit themselves to formal education, the world class is open to anything that moves them closer to their goals.

Rich Resource:

▶ *Get a Financial Life: Personal Finance in Your Twenties and Thirties* by Beth Kobliner

Critical Thinking Question:

▶ What are you doing on a daily basis to further educate yourself on how to become wealthy?

Action Step:

▶ Join a referral marketing or direct sales company with a multilevel compensation plan to learn how to sell products, recruit people, and build a team. You will learn more about how rich people think and operate from observing the top performers in these companies than anywhere else I've found in twenty-six years of research.

"They know enough who know how to learn."

—HENRY ADAMS

12

Middle Class Believes Money Is Earned through Labor, World Class Believes Money Is Earned through Thought

THE AVERAGE PERSON BELIEVES THE HARDER THEY WORK, THE MORE MONEY THEY'LL MAKE. Their linear thinking equates labor and effort with financial success. This is why most people aren't rich. They're following an outdated model of success and are confounded when they reach middle age with little money to show for twenty years of hard work. The rich know that creative thinking is the highest paid skill in the world. Independent, creative thinking is the most valuable asset anyone can acquire. So while the masses are trying to figure out how to put their kids through college and retire on half of what they can barely exist on now, the great ones are building empires, living in abundance, and donating large sums to their favorite causes.

This sets off a psychological domino effect, because once a person thinks and lives at this level of abundance, they know even greater levels of success are possible through the vehicle of creative thought. Most of us were told as kids that if we paid attention in school, got good grades, and went to a respectable college or university, our success was virtually guaranteed. The reality is few people who follow this formula ever get rich. They survive, and some become the most successful people in their families. But world-class wealth is rarely achieved by people who follow this model. The rich eventually figure out that training your mind to find solutions to difficult problems is the real secret to making money. The good news is this is possible for anyone who conditions their mind to think this way, and then transforms thought into action.

Rich Resource:

▶ *Simple Wealth, Inevitable Wealth: How You and Your Financial Advisor Can Grow Your Fortune in Stock Mutual Funds* by Nick Murray

Critical Thinking Question:

▶ How much time do you invest on a weekly basis in self-education?

Action Step:

▶ Commit to investing at least one hour per day studying subjects that will help you move closer to your ultimate vision.

"The real source of wealth and capital in this new era is not material things. It is the human mind, the human spirit, the human imagination, and our faith in the future."

—STEVE FORBES

Middle Class Worries about Running Out of Money, World Class Thinks about How to Make More Money

POOR PEOPLE SPEND MORE TIME THINKING ABOUT MONEY THAN RICH PEOPLE. The problem is poor people spend this time worrying about what they'll do if they lose their job, get sick, or exceed their budget through poor planning or bad luck. Most of this worry is a waste of time, not to mention the negative, destructive psychological impact it has on their minds and the physiological havoc it wreaks with their bodies. Living in fear isn't living; it's surviving.

World-class performers find problems that are profitable to solve and spend most of their time focused on solving them. They know money will follow the solution, so logic dictates they direct their mental energy toward creative and critical thought, which is rooted in the belief that just because a solution hasn't been discovered doesn't mean it doesn't exist. No fear lives at this level of consciousness. Creative critical thinking is the highest form of thought and is single-handedly responsible for all progress in the history of civilization. Every product or service that has made our lives better has come from creative thought.

So when I say the world class thinks about how to make more money, what they're actually thinking about is creative problem solving, not money itself. Wealthy people are often criticized for being obsessed with money, but the truth is it's the poor, working, and middle classes that spend the most time thinking about it. If the masses would upgrade their limiting beliefs about money and redirect their mental energy to new and exciting ideas, they would experience financial abundance. Money flows to great ideas like water. The secret is learning how to turn on the faucet.

Rich Resource:

▶ *The Everything Investing Book: Make Money, Plan Ahead, and Secure Your Financial Future!* by Michele Cagan CPA and Brian O'Connell

Critical Thinking Question:

▶ How much time do you spend worrying about money compared to the time you spend engaged in creative problem solving?

Action Step:

▶ Identify the biggest problem in your business or industry that, if solved, would earn you a fortune. Then go solve it.

"Money never starts an idea; it is the idea that starts the money."

—WILLIAM J. CAMERON

Middle Class Thinks about Spending, World Class Thinks about Investing

THE MIDDLE CLASS IS FAMOUS FOR LIVING BEYOND THEIR MEANS. They're not spendthrifts, but they earn so little that they have to spend it all to live a decent existence. To further exacerbate their frustration, they're scolded by financial experts who insist they discipline themselves and trim their spending. This is sound but middle-class advice. The world-class answer is to double or triple your income and create enough wealth so you can enjoy the good life to your heart's desire without worries. This way, you can join the wealthy and focus on investing the remainder of your money in stocks, bonds, real estate, art, and any other wealth-building vehicle you choose.

The rich get richer because they know the world is overflowing with wealth disguised as problems that need to be solved. They know any free-market economy will gladly make them as rich as they desire in exchange for solutions to problems. The bigger the problems you solve, the wealthier society will make you. The more people who benefit from your ideas, the more abundance you receive in return. The more you have to invest, the more your money goes to work for you, even as you sleep. That's another reason the rich get richer: they've learned how to make money work for them twenty-four hours a day. And it's not because they're investing every penny. The rich like to spend and enjoy their money like everyone else. It's that they have so much of it, there's always plenty to invest. So instead of focusing on spending and saving, focus on how to earn more, invest a percentage, and spend the remainder any way you wish.

You only live once and you can't take it with you. Why not enjoy it?

Rich Resource:

▶   *How to Build Wealth* by Peter Suchy

Critical Thinking Question:

▶   How much time do you invest in increasing your ability to earn more money compared to the time you spend watching television or surfing the internet?

Action Step:

▶   Decide to double your income in the next two to five years. You don't have to know how to do it yet. The first step is to decide to make it happen.

"Old men are always advising young men to save money. That is bad advice. Don't save every nickel. Invest in yourself."

—HENRY FORD

15

Middle Class Focuses on Pleasurable Activities, World Class Focuses on Money-Making Activities

THE MASSES SPEND A SUBSTANTIAL AMOUNT OF TIME ENTERTAINING THEMSELVES IN A VARIETY OF ACTIVITIES. They live in a state of consciousness where effort is minimal and pleasure is king. Billion-dollar industries are created overnight when smart marketers give the masses what they want most: comfort and entertainment. Rich people focus the majority of their attention on money-making activities they enjoy. They parlay a love for real estate into property speculation, a passion for beautiful paintings into investment art, or a flair for numbers into buying and selling stocks. So while they're working, they're making money, and while they're enjoying their hobbies, they're still making money. Wealthy people know leverage is one of the great secrets of success, and they go to great lengths to employ it. While the masses are memorizing box scores and batting averages, the world class is directing the same amount of mental energy into revenue-producing ideas.

To the average person, it looks like the rich are working all the time, but one of the smartest strategies of the world class is doing what they love and finding a way to get paid for it. The world class is famous for saying that the best thing about being rich is you never have to do anything you don't want to do, and this includes how they earn money. The critical thinking question is which comes first: doing what you love, or making money to ensure you have the choice? While either way will work, the majority of wealthy people

I've interviewed over the past twenty-six years didn't make serious money until they were doing what they loved. Over and over they've told me the same thing: when you're doing what you love, you think about it twenty-four hours a day. Anything that has that much laser-focused mental energy directed toward it is going to produce massive success.

Rich Resource:

▶ *You Were Born Rich: Now You Can Discover and Develop Those Riches* by Bob Proctor

Critical Thinking Question:

▶ What would you love to do for a living more than anything else?

Action Step:

▶ Do some research and find out if anyone is making a living doing what you'd love to do.

"Wealth flows from
energy and ideas."
—WILLIAM FEATHER

16

Middle Class Sees Money as a Finite Resource, World Class Sees Money as an Infinite Resource

THE AVERAGE PERSON BELIEVES THERE'S A LIMITED AMOUNT OF MONEY AND THAT THEY NEED TO STRUGGLE AND FIGHT FOR THEIR SHARE BEFORE SOMEONE ELSE GETS IT. They live in a world of fear and scarcity that says money is hard to make and harder to keep. Due to years of middle-class programming, their negative and limiting relationship with money almost guarantees they will never accumulate more than a modest net worth.

Once again, the rich occupy the opposite side of

the spectrum. Although most of them had the same middle-class, fear-based programming in childhood, somewhere along the way, they were able to reprogram their beliefs and develop a healthy relationship with money. The rich understand money flows from ideas, and since ideas are limitless, money is limitless. So while the masses are directing their mental energy toward grabbing as much money as they can, the great ones are focused on creating new ideas that have the potential of generating abundant wealth.

The rich use money to fuel their passions and bring their dreams to life. It's not the money they crave: it's living life on their terms without the interference of others. The middle class has always criticized the world class for being greedy, ruthless, and materialistic, and there is a segment of successful people that fits this description, known as the upper class. These people are driven by blind ambition and killer instinct. If you get in their way, they will run you over without hesitation. But the world class is different. The world class is spirit-centered, and they are among the most caring, compassionate people. These are the folks who provide the majority of the funding for the great charities and nonprofit causes. They know how to use money to improve or advance anything they care about. The reason they aren't afraid to give is they know money is in infinite supply. If they need more, they simply use their minds to create more.

Welcome to the world of the self-made rich. A world they create with their minds. A world of unlimited abundance. If they can do it, why can't you?

Rich Resource:

▶ *Wealth Secrets of the Affluent: Keys to Fortune Building and Asset Protection* by Christopher R. Jarvis and David B. Mandell

Critical Thinking Question:

▶ Do you believe that since there is an infinite supply of ideas, your earning potential is unlimited?

Action Step:

▶ Make a list of the five major beliefs you have about money that you know are true...and challenge the validity of each one.

"Every person who gets rich by creation opens a way for thousands to follow—and inspires them to do so."

—WALLACE D. WATTLES

Middle Class Earns Money Doing Things They Don't Like to Do, World Class Gets Rich Doing What They Love

THE AVERAGE PERSON FINDS A JOB OR CAREER THEY CAN TOLERATE AND STICKS WITH IT FOR YEARS WHILE DREAMING OF RETIREMENT. In recent years, people have held multiple jobs with different companies and even changed occupations, but the mindset of the masses hasn't changed. The majority of people drag themselves to a job they don't like while simultaneously worrying about getting fired. They don't do this because they're stupid; they do it because they need the money and they've been trained in school and conditioned by society to live in a linear-thinking world that equates earning money with physical or mental effort.

The rich have retrained themselves to operate in a nonlinear consciousness where anything is possible. The greatest example of this nonlinear concept is the idea that passion is the real secret of getting rich. It's a cause-and-effect relationship between effort and passion—but while the masses see passion as the effect, the great ones see it as the cause. In other words, the average person goes to work every day and hopes to find passion in his or her efforts. The rich go to work every day feeling passion for what they do, and their passion fuels their efforts. This is not a semantic argument; it's a personal philosophy and strategy that serves as the foundation for every great fortune ever earned. There's been an attempt to bring this mindset to the masses by espousing the world-class philosophy of "do what you love and the money will follow." There was even a book written by that exact title. The sad

truth is only a small percentage of the population will ever adopt this philosophy.

Years of fear, scarcity-based programming, and daily reinforcement of a lack-and-limitation mentality will prevent most people from ever entering the world of the wealthy. While that fact is tough to dispute, it has nothing to do with you and me. We know the truth. We know we were sold a bill of goods in childhood by well-meaning adults who could only give us the best they had. You and I know it's not enough, and the good news is that all of our middle-class beliefs can be upgraded or eliminated. We are in complete control, and that makes our futures limitless. The first world-class belief about wealth you must adopt is that it's possible to do what you love and get rich doing it. Once this belief is established, anything is possible, because you're now cognitively cohabiting with the wealthy in a state of consciousness the masses don't even know exists.

Rich Resource:

▶ *The Last Chance Millionaire: It's Not Too Late to Become Wealthy* by Douglas R. Andrew

Critical Thinking Question:

▶ Do you believe it's possible to build your financial empire doing what you love to do?

Action Step:

▶ Talk to a couple people who seem to be doing what they love while living a fabulous lifestyle, and ask them how they did it.

"Rule No. 1: Never lose money. Rule No. 2: Never forget rule No. 1"

—WARREN BUFFETT

Middle Class Has a Lottery Mentality, World Class Has an Action Mentality

THE MASSES LOVE THE LOTTERY BECAUSE DEEP DOWN THEY BELIEVE IT'S THEIR ONLY CHANCE TO GET RICH. The fact is, they're probably right. Not because they're not capable, but because they don't have faith in their own abilities, and their beliefs about money limit their financial success.

The middle class is self-destructive, especially when it comes to money. They will always struggle financially unless they are somehow able to break the mold cast

in childhood telling them only crooks and lucky people get rich. The world class has empowering beliefs about money that leads them to effective daily action that serves as the foundation of their financial success. The great ones know that talk is cheap and that the only way to get wealthy is to take action.

On the surface, the distinction between the classes seems simple, but it is actually counterintuitive. Understanding the cause-and-effect relationship is what gives it clarity. Many people believe, as I used to, that the masses do not possess the raw desire to get rich and therefore never take the necessary steps. The truth is, they have all the desire they need, but they lack the beliefs that would wake their latent desire. The cause of their inaction is not lack of desire but lack of empowering beliefs regarding the acquisition of money. Beliefs dictate behavior, and behavior dictates results. That's what the rich understand that the middle class doesn't. If you want to get rich, dissect your beliefs about money and upgrade them to world class. Once you've taken care of the cause, the effect will follow, and you'll start moving toward wealth because you will be thinking like a rich person.

When the rich need money, they don't wonder if it's possible; they simply begin creating new ideas that solve problems. They don't waste mental energy worrying or wondering about their ability to produce cash; they direct their concentration toward creative thinking. Do you see why this is so effective? Do you understand now why the rich get richer? Do you see how you can do the exact same thing? The rich aren't any smarter than us. They are just more strategic.

Rich Resource:

▶ *Rich Dad, Poor Dad: What the Rich Teach Their Kids about Money That the Poor and Middle Class Do Not!* by Robert Kiyosaki

Critical Thinking Question:

▶ On a scale of one to seven, seven being strongest, how strong is your desire to be rich?

Action Step:

▶ To stoke your desire, create a written vision for what you want your life to look like five years from now.

1 9B 3

11:18:03:18

Picr Connectiom	1/25/16
Leo Zhuchenko	A	23.976
Avel Chuklanov		INT

"It requires a great deal of boldness and a great deal of caution to make a great fortune, and when you have it, it requires ten times as much skill to keep it."

—RALPH WALDO EMERSON

Middle Class Is Waiting to Be Rescued from Financial Mediocrity, World Class Knows No One Is Coming to the Rescue

THE MIDDLE CLASS LIVES IN A PERPETUAL WAITING GAME FOR OUTSIDE FORCES TO COME TO THEIR AID AND GRANT THEIR EVERY WISH. Whether it's losing weight and getting fit, enhancing their relationships, or getting rich, they are operating at a level of consciousness that encourages them to wait passively for life to improve. The hero they're waiting for may be God, the government, their boss, or their spouse. It's the average person's level of thinking that breeds this approach to life and living while the clock keeps ticking away. The number-one regret people have on their deathbed is: "I should have taken more risks." The greatest risk you can take is playing it safe while expecting to get what you want. The great ones know that no one is coming to the rescue, and they are glad. Any world-class performer will tell you that it's not getting what you want that's so much fun, but the person you become along the journey.

World-class performers who get rich are the happiest people I've interviewed over the last twenty-six years, but they're not happy because they're rich. Their happiness stems from setting a goal, fighting the fight, and winning the game. The money is just a measuring stick of their mindset. Money makes their life easier and more comfortable. The money gives them opportunities to do and see things most people never experience. But the money doesn't make them happy. Money and happiness have little to do with each other. Money is just a tool of exchange. Happiness is an emotional

experience. The two have almost nothing in common. They're both important, yet largely unrelated.

The ego-driven upper class has always believed riches will bring them happiness, which is why they are often emotionally tortured. These are the most miserable people I've ever interviewed, yet many are super rich. What they counted on to finally make their lives fulfilling barely made an impact, and they are often confounded by this phenomenon. Unfortunately, this is a group of rich people the media likes to report on often, and it sends the message to society that getting rich makes people miserable. What they're missing is an elevated level of consciousness that must accompany the wealth if a person is going to be happy, and that consciousness is the spirit-driven, love, and abundance-living world class. And it all starts with a self-reliant mindset that refuses to wait for outside forces or circumstances to make things happen.

Rich Resource:

▶ *The Automatic Millionaire: A Powerful One-Step Plan to Live and Finish Rich* by David Bach

Critical Thinking Question:

▶ Are you taking daily action toward getting rich or waiting to be rescued?

Action Step:

▶ Create a daily plan of action that will move you closer to building financial independence.

"Don't let the opinions of the average man sway you. Dream, and he thinks you're crazy. Succeed, and he thinks you're lucky. Acquire wealth, and he thinks you're greedy. Pay no attention. He simply doesn't understand."

—ROBERT G. ALLEN

20

Middle Class Believes Money Changes People, World Class Believes Money Reveals People

CONTRARY TO POPULAR BELIEF, MONEY IS NOT THE CATALYST OF CORRUPTION. Money is a force for good. The average person has a set of beliefs and philosophies that say success and money turn people into greedy, corrupt, uncaring oppressors. It's another in a long list of limiting beliefs that keeps people from getting rich. It's also used as an excuse by and for those people who claim moral and ethical superiority but who struggle along on a paycheck-to-paycheck existence.

Champions know that any kind of power, freedom, or liberation reveals the true person. If you were a crook or a cheater before you were rich, you'll be worse when you're wealthy. If you were an honest, hardworking, humble person before, you'll be even better with expanded resources. Getting rich is one of the catalysts that liberates and reveals a person's true self. The masses love to blame money for as many things as possible, because it psychologically absolves them from the responsibility of acquiring it. After all, we want to be good people, right? The saddest part of this trap is that most who fall into it can't see how ridiculous it is and how it virtually guarantees they will struggle and suffer for money their entire lives. Meanwhile, the rich continue getting richer, being who they always were.

Rich Resource:

▶ *Mind Over Money: Overcoming the Money Disorders That Threaten Our Financial Health* by Brad Klontz and Ted Klontz

Critical Thinking Question:

▶ Do you believe getting rich will bring out the best or the worst in you?

Action Step:

▶ Write down the ten things you like best about yourself, and promise yourself you won't ever allow being rich to weaken your character.

"Money will make you more of what you already are. If you're not a nice person, money's going to make you a despicable individual. If you're a good person, money's going to make you a better person."

—BOB PROCTOR

21

Middle Class Believes in Working for Money, World Class Believes in Working for Fulfillment

THE MASSES HAVE BEEN HANDING DOWN BAD ADVICE ABOUT THE OCCUPATION-MONEY RELATIONSHIP FOR CENTURIES. Their philosophy is to spend the majority of your waking hours toiling away for the sole purpose of economic survival, while being grateful for the opportunity. With the exception of times when this was the best society had to offer, it's not only a bad strategy for accumulating wealth, but also a terrible road map for life in general. In modern day America, and every other free-market economy, this way of thinking assaults the human spirit. The rich have always known working for the sole purpose of making money is the worst strategy for building wealth. The great ones go through an extensive introspective soul-searching process to discover what they love to do and combine it with their unique talents and abilities. These people appear to be working hard, but the truth is they're not working at all! They're doing something they would do for free because they love it.

My late business partner, the great Bill Gove, was known around the world as the father of professional speaking. One of the greatest pieces of wisdom I heard him deliver from stages all over the world was this: "When you're doing something you love to do, the only reward you need is the experience of doing it." The wonderful paradox of this wisdom is that when you're doing something you love and you're very good at it, the world will gladly make you rich. Instead of setting out to find work with the most profit potential, focus on work that has the most fulfillment potential. Once you find it, invest so much heart and soul into your work that you become one of the most competent people in your field. You'll be rewarded with uncommon wealth.

The root cause in the approach of the masses and the wealthy is the level of consciousness each operates from: the middle class, from fear and scarcity; the world class, from love and abundance. This difference in consciousness leads one group to seek survival and the other to manifest dreams. The only question that really matters is: which group are you in?

Rich Resource:

▶ *The Debt-Free Millionaire: Winning Strategies to Creating Great Credit and Retiring Rich* by Anthony Manganiello

Critical Thinking Question:

▶ On a scale of one to seven, seven being most fulfilling, how fulfilling is your current occupation?

Action Step:

▶ If you didn't rate a seven on this question, set a goal to be doing what you would love to do in the next twelve to twenty-four months. No excuses. You can do it!

"A man is a success if he gets up in the morning and gets to bed at night, and in between he does what he wants to do."

—BOB DYLAN

22

Middle Class Believes You Have to Have Money to Make Money, World Class Believes in Using Other People's Money

THE MAJORITY OF THE WORLD'S POPULATION IS OPERATING FROM A CONSCIOUSNESS ROOTED IN LINEAR THINKING. An example is in their approach to earning money. Linear thinking tells them if they work more hours they'll make more money, and that's true. It's also the most inefficient way to earn more money and another reason most people don't have much. The rich are masters of nonlinear thinking, especially as it relates to money. An example is in how they create an idea they are unable to finance and then proceed to use other people's money to make it happen.

The most frequently uttered comment of the middle class in reference to money is "I can't afford it." Rich people know not being solvent enough to personally afford something is not relevant. The real question is: "Is this worth buying, investing in, or pursuing?" If so, the wealthy know money is always available because rich people are always looking for great investments and superior performers to make those investments profitable. The great ones are aware that it's easier to borrow ten million dollars than ten thousand, a critical nonlinear concept to know when raising capital. Like a serious hunter stalking big game, savvy investors like large numbers and exciting deals they can sink their teeth into while expanding their empires.

The middle-class cliché that you have to have money to make money is limiting at best and destructive at worst. The truth is you have to have great ideas that solve problems to make money. If you do, you

will attract money like a magnet. Money is only an instrument of exchange. Creative ideas are the scarce resource, but most people are so focused on where the money is coming from that they ignore their ideas, yet the ideas are the only thing that will actually attract the money in the first place! Are you starting to see why a tiny percentage of the population owns the majority of the world's wealth? Are you starting to see that it's completely in your power to join them?

Rich Resource:

▶ *The Motley Fool Investment Guide: How The Fool Beats Wall Street's Wise Men and How You Can Too* by David Gardner and Tom Gardner

Critical Thinking Question:

▶ Do you have a big idea you can't personally finance but that has the potential to capture the attention of outside investors?

Action Step:

▶ Write down ten of your biggest and best business and investment ideas and select your favorite to court potential investors.

"No one can become rich without enriching others. Anyone who adds to prosperity must prosper in turn."

—G. ALEXANDER ORNDORFF

Middle Class Believes Jobs Are the Safest Way to Earn Money, World Class Believes Outstanding Performance Is the Safest Way to Earn Money

THE AVERAGE PERSON GROWING UP IN THE UNITED STATES IS BOMBARDED WITH THE SAME MESSAGE: GET A GOOD EDUCATION SO YOU CAN GET A GOOD JOB. Interesting advice in a country founded and established on the ideals of independence, entrepreneurship, and freedom. It is not that there aren't world-class performers who punch a time clock for a paycheck, but for most, this is the slowest path to prosperity, promoted as the safest. The truth is having a job is no safer than owning a business.

As counterintuitive as this may seem, people who work for themselves have the power to proactively seek out business and increase revenues at will. They can work as many or few hours as they wish and change the direction of the company any time they choose. They are not subject to the whims of management or the politics of corporate culture. The self-employed are the architects of their own destiny.

But while the middle class is attracted to jobs for safety, the world class knows the only safety any service or product provider has lies in her ability to perform. No matter who signs your paycheck, your financial success will always be based on the level of service you provide and how many people you provide it to. The great ones know there's no such thing as safety in a free-market economy. Labor unions, human resources departments, and lawsuits initiated by poor-performing employees are becoming less effective in an increasingly competitive, performance-driven marketplace. This is where world-class performers

seize the opportunity to get rich while the middle class makes a mediocre effort and hides behind the perceived protection of the corporate structure. There are people with jobs who get rich, but the percentage is small. The fastest way to wealth is to work for yourself and determine the size of your own paycheck. The greatest form of security is to have millions in the bank. The rich take advantage of this, while the masses wait on the sidelines, terrified to get in the game for fear they will lose the little money they have. Meanwhile, the world class is earning more in a year than the average person will make in a lifetime, and the heart of the reason is the unwillingness to let go of a security that does not actually exist.

Rich Resource:

▶ *The One Minute Millionaire: The Enlightened Way to Wealth* by Mark Victor Hansen and Robert G. Allen

Critical Thinking Question:

▶ Are you trading your opportunity to get rich for a false sense of security?

Action Step:

▶ Do a personal and professional risk assessment on your finances and career. You may discover that starting a business is less risky than you think.

"Too many people are thinking of security instead of opportunity. They seem more afraid of life than of death."

—JAMES F. BYRNES

24

Middle Class Believes in Financial Scarcity, World Class Believes in Financial Abundance

AS CHILDREN, WE ALL HEARD THE SAYING "MONEY DOESN'T GROW ON TREES." This programs people to believe that making money is hard and that there's a limited amount of it. The rich understand their relationship with money as one of unlimited abundance, based on fair exchange.

Figuratively speaking, money does grow on trees, and the trees are ideas. As long as man walks the earth, he will have problems that need to be solved by creative ideas. And the more problems the performer solves, the richer she becomes. So, while the average person is operating from the faulty belief that money is scarce and difficult to earn, the rich are operating on the belief that money is abundant and that earning it is as easy as solving a problem through persistent, creative thought. This is why world-class thinking is the most valuable skill you can acquire.

The masses are conditioned from one generation to the next to hoard their money and pray they don't run out before they die. This "playing not to lose" strategy guarantees a life of fear and scarcity. The rich see this as preposterous, if not plain stupid. But to a fear-based thinker whose top priorities are safety, security, and comfort, it makes perfect sense. This strategy offers little hope of acquiring substantial net worth, and few realize they dug their own financial graves years before when they bought into a series of middle-class beliefs that would limit them forever.

The masses think getting rich is primarily external,

while the world class knows it's an inside game. Few people ever get rich operating out of a fear- and scarcity-based consciousness. Those who do rarely enjoy it, because they are always afraid of losing what they have. Fear-based thinking attaches itself to everything that enters your mind. The good news is love- and abundance-based thinking does the same thing, so the trick is to program yourself to believe in the never-ending abundance of money. This is backed up and proven by the philosophy stating that if money flows to ideas that solve problems, and ideas are limitless, money must be limitless. Once you understand the impact of this philosophy and integrate it into your consciousness, you are on your way to a life of economic prosperity most people only see in movies.

Rich Resource:

▶ *Spend Well, Live Rich: How to Get What You Want with the Money You Have* by Michelle Singletary

Critical Thinking Question:

▶ Do you believe you have the potential to earn as much money as you wish? If not, why not? If so, do your actions reflect your belief?

Action Step:

▶ How much money is enough for you? Identify your number and create a plan to achieve it. You can always adjust your number and your plan as you evolve.

"If a person gets his attitude toward money straight, it will help straighten out almost every other area in his life."

—BILLY GRAHAM

25

Middle Class Believes They Aren't Worthy of Great Wealth, World Class Believes They Deserve to Be Rich

THERE IS A PERVASIVE BELIEF AMONG THE MASSES THAT TELLS THEM THEY DON'T HAVE THE RIGHT NOR ARE THEY GOOD ENOUGH AS HUMAN BEINGS TO ASK, HOPE, OR PRAY FOR PROSPERITY BEYOND THEIR BASIC NEEDS. "Who am I," they ask themselves, "to become a millionaire? Who am I to get what I really want? Who am I to live a lifestyle fit for a king?" The world class asks, "Why not me? I'm as good as anyone else, and I deserve to be rich. If I serve others by solving problems, why shouldn't I be rewarded with a fortune?" And since they have this belief, their behavior moves them toward the manifestation of their dreams. Whether they actually deserve to be rich is irrelevant. Like all beliefs, they don't have to be true to be acted on.

While scholars and philosophers debate whether any of us has the right to be rich in a world where people are starving, the world class continues moving closer to the level of prosperity they have convinced themselves they deserve. This is why some of the smartest people are among the poorest, while people of average intelligence build fortunes through their beliefs, positive expectations, and focus. If teachers, college professors, and other educational experts fully understood this, would there be anyone left to teach? Most likely, but only the teachers who love the profession and would do it for free if they could afford to. Whether you believe you deserve to be rich or not, you are right. Philosophers have been pondering this question for centuries, and the debate will continue long after we are gone. Base your belief on the result you want to accomplish. If you can choose to be rich, why would you settle for mediocrity? Do you really believe God, the universe, or any higher power will reward you for squandering your opportunities?

Rich Resource:

▶ *The Little Book of Bull Moves in Bear Markets: How to Keep Your Portfolio Up When the Market Is Down* by Peter D. Schiff

Critical Thinking Question:

▶ If you are willing and able to provide world-class service to others, don't you deserve to be compensated with world-class wealth?

Action Step:

▶ Ask your five closest friends this question: Do you deserve to be rich? Their answers may surprise you.

"Man was born to be rich, or, inevitably grows rich by the use of his faculties."

—RALPH WALDO EMERSON

26

Middle Class Believes Money Is Their Enemy, World Class Believes Money Is Their Friend

THE MASSES HAVE A DYSFUNCTIONAL, ADVERSARIAL RELATIONSHIP WITH MONEY. We are taught that money is scarce, hard to earn, and harder to keep. People of influence in childhood instructed us to work hard and hoard as much money as possible. Teachers, coaches, parents, clergy, and other authority figures, most of whom had little money, conditioned us to see money as a necessary evil. The world class has the same child-hood experience but, along the way, had exposure to a higher thought level that changed the way they think about wealth. They learn that money is not the enemy, but one of their greatest allies and friends. It is a friend that has the power to end sleepless nights of worry, physical pain, and even save their life. They learn that money is not materialistic; people are materialistic. Money is just a medium of exchange without attachment to anything good or bad. Blaming money for greed and materialism is like blaming food for making people fat. It's delusional thinking. The rich see money as a special friend that can help them in ways no other friend can, and these positive feelings lead them to build a stronger relationship every day. The more money you acquire, the more you understand it, and the more you understand it, the more good you can do with it. The great ones continue to cultivate and nurture their relationship with money by thinking about how to earn more, invest wiser, and leverage as much as possible. The rich do this so well that they often acquire much more money than they'll ever want or need, which is typically when they turn their attention to giving the excess away to charitable organizations. These groups wouldn't survive without the success and generosity of the wealthy who have adopted money as a close friend.

Rich Resource:

▶ *Investing in Gold: The Essential Safe Haven Investment for Every Portfolio* by Jonathan Spall

Critical Thinking Question:

▶ Do you see money as your friend or as something you wish you didn't have to think about?

Action Step:

▶ Start telling yourself on a daily basis that money is your friend and a positive force in your life, and your mind will go to work to help you acquire more.

"Money, which represents the prose of life, and which is hardly spoken of in parlors without an apology, is, in its effects and laws, as beautiful as roses."

—RALPH WALDO EMERSON

Middle Class Lives Beyond Their Means, World Class Lives Below Their Means

THE AVERAGE PERSON SPENDS MORE THAN THEY MAKE BECAUSE THEY MAKE SO LITTLE. How can a family survive on the average income and still save money? The greatest financial wizard in the world couldn't pull that off! Instead of getting creative, most people try to do more with less and suffer sleepless nights worrying about the future. If this were a fringe group in society, I wouldn't mention it. But it's not. It's the majority of the population living in the richest country in the history of civilization! The middle class is the wealthiest subgroup of the working poor, and most of them live beyond their means because they earn so little. These people aren't stupid; to the contrary, some are smarter and better educated than members of the world class. The difference lies in their focus. The middle class focuses on everything but getting wealthy because they have so many limiting beliefs about money and what being wealthy means; it's the last thing they want to think about. Then they listen to so-called financial gurus who berate them for overspending on frivolous things. The rich live below their means, not because they're so savvy, but because they make so much money, they can afford to live like royalty while still having a king's ransom socked away for the future. It's easy to live below your means when you earn more in a day than most people earn in a year. Not to mention that the rich earn money primarily through leverage and not hard labor. It's hard labor that creates the physical and psychological stress that kills so many poverty-, working-, and middle-class workers. Here's how to live below your means and tap into the secret wealthy people have used for centuries: get so rich you can afford to.

Rich Resource:

▶ *24 Essential Lessons for Investment Success: Learn the Most Important Investment Techniques from the Founder of* Investor's Business Daily by William J. O'Neil

Critical Thinking Question:

▶ How much money would you have to earn in a year to live the way you want to?

Action Step:

▶ Decide how much money you would ultimately like to spend, save, and invest every year, and map out a plan and a deadline to make it happen.

"There is no dignity quite so impressive, and no independence quite so important, as living within your means."

—CALVIN COOLIDGE

28

Middle Class Dreams of Having Enough Money to Retire, World Class Dreams of Having Enough Money to Impact the World

WHEN I BEGAN STUDYING THE ULTRASUCCESSFUL AND SUPERRICH IN 1984, I THOUGHT THEY WERE MORE AMBITIOUS THAN THE AVERAGE PERSON. I later discovered after hundreds of interviews that it wasn't the lack of desire that held the masses back from getting wealthy, but the lack of belief in their own ability to make it happen. The average person is carrying around so many limiting beliefs about money it's a miracle they acquire any at all. Without some intervention, lucky break, or exposure to a book like this, most people have little or no chance of ever becoming rich. The sad thing is, they have everything they need to make more money than they can spend, and without the interference of a slew of middle-class beliefs, they would accomplish it.

The problem is that outside the consciousness-expanding world of personal development, the masses are never taught the power beliefs have on our behaviors and results. Beliefs literally control everything we do unless they are interrupted consciously through free will or upgraded through programming. This is common knowledge among behavioral science professionals and experts who study the mind, but the general public is oblivious to it. Their fear and scarcity-based thinking leads them to look at everything through the filters of skepticism and cynicism as a protective mechanism. This holds them back from studying life-changing books and attending belief-altering seminars led by thought leaders in the field.

As a result of this limited thinking, the masses' major

goal with money is to retire at sixty-five and hopefully have enough money to survive until they die. The world class, while often no more ambitious, set their sights on impacting the world with their wealth. Some do it through philanthropy; others through business or various financial vehicles. They do all of this while living the good life materially and enjoying the peace of mind that comes along with being rich.

Rich Resource:

▶ *Money Management for Those Who Don't Have Any* by James L. Paris

Critical Thinking Question:

▶ If you were a millionaire, what would you do to make a positive impact on the world?

Action Step:

▶ Make a list of five ways you could make a difference for other people if you had the money, and estimate approximately how much it would cost.

"Wealth is power. With wealth many things are possible."

—GEORGE CLASON

Middle Class Sees the Wealthy as Oppressors, World Class Sees the Wealthy as Liberators

THE MIDDLE CLASS HAS AND WILL ALWAYS SERVE THE WORLD CLASS. This reality, combined with a fear-based consciousness, leads the masses to feel envy and jealousy toward the rich and powerful. The wealthy employ the working poor and middle class, and this gives the average person the feeling that their employers are their oppressors. World-class thinkers see the rich as the great liberators of society in part because they pay the most taxes, donate the most to charity,

and create products, services, and companies that employ the masses. Whenever there's a national crisis or financial emergency, leaders look to the rich to save the day by raising taxes, leveraging their contacts or political favors, or pleading for their compassion to help solve a situation only a rich person can solve.

Another reason the rich are the great liberators of society is because they have the ability to make choices and move ideas. The average person barely has enough financial power to stay ahead of the bill collector. Even in the richest country in the world, the majority of the population is one paycheck away from living on the street. This reality keeps them operating in fear-based thinking, which perpetuates the beliefs, philosophies, and behaviors that got them where they are in the first place. Meanwhile, the rich are operating in a mindset of love, abundance, and gratitude and continue getting wealthier every day. This experience perpetuates the cycle of success that becomes a self-fulfilling prophecy until the performer believes he is capable of achieving any goal or dream he can imagine. While both groups are living in the same outer world, their inner world is on a different psychological plane. The more time goes by, the more the gap widens.

Rich Resource:

▶ *Your Money or Your Life: 9 Steps to Transforming Your Relationship with Money and Achieving Financial Independence: Revised and Updated for the 21st Century* by Vicki Robin and Joe Dominguez, with Monique Tilford

Critical Thinking Question:

▶ When you were growing up, were you taught that rich people were liberators or oppressors? Were rich people portrayed as more negative or positive?

Action Step:

▶ Make a list of ten reasons rich people are a positive influence on society.

"Don't knock the rich. When did a poor person give you a job?"

—LAURENCE J. PETER

30

Middle Class Believes Getting Rich Is Outside Their Control, World Class Knows Getting Rich Is an Inside Job

THE MASSES DO NOT UNDERSTAND THE NATURE OF BUILD-
ING WEALTH, WHICH IS WHY GENERATION AFTER GENERA-
TION APPROACHES IT THE SAME WAY AND ALMOST ALWAYS
FAILS. Schools teach the basics of balancing a check-
book, adhering to a budget, and basic math. This
trains children and young adults to think about money
in linear, logical terms, which can seal their fate financially before they earn their high school diploma. Unless
they are exposed to the truth about building wealth

through a book like this, a speaker who challenges them at a personal development seminar, or a rich mentor, the game is over before it begins.

The fact is that getting rich begins with the way you think and what you believe about making money. If your parents were broke or in the middle class, you might end up the same if you were to adopt their beliefs and philosophies about money. Critical thinking says the only reason people settle for a mediocre, middle-class existence is because they are unaware of how to move beyond it. The secret has always been the same: thinking. The only way to learn how to think like a rich person is to study them. Every action we take stems from the way we think and what we believe. While the masses believe becoming wealthy is out of their control, the world class knows earning money and amassing wealth is a cause-and-effect relationship. The cause of our behavior is our belief system; the effect of our behavior is the result we get. Change the cause, and by default, you automatically change the behavior and bottom-line result. Knowing this, the world-class thinker is always upgrading her beliefs and philosophies on money by studying those who are wealthier.

Rich Resource:

▶ *Please Send Money: A Financial Survival Guide for Young Adults on Their Own* by Dara Duguay

Critical Thinking Question:

▶ Do you think like the rich?

Action Step:

▶ Based on what you've learned in this book, make a list of five beliefs rich people have about money and begin telling yourself you believe these things too.

"Wealth is largely a result of habit."

—JOHN JACOB ASTOR

ABOUT THE AUTHOR

STEVE SIEBOLD IS A FORMER PROFESSIONAL ATHLETE AND NATIONAL COACH. He's spent the past twenty-six years studying the thought processes, habits, and philosophies of world-class performers. Today, he helps Fortune 500 companies increase sales through mental toughness training. His clients include Johnson & Johnson, Toyota, and Procter & Gamble. *How Rich People Think* is his fifth book on mental toughness. His national television show, *Mental Toughness with Steve*

Siebold, won the 2007 Telly Award for best motivational show. Steve has appeared on *The Today Show*, *Good Morning America*, ABC News, FOX, CBS, TBS, BBC, NBC Australia, and dozens of others. As a professional speaker, Steve ranks among the top 1 percent of income earners worldwide. Steve's blog, mentaltoughnessblog.com, is one of the fastest-growing personal development video blogs on the internet, with thousands of subscribers around the globe.

Steve has been married since 1986 to Dawn Andrews. The couple spends summers on Lake Lanier in northern Georgia and winters in Palm Beach County, Florida.

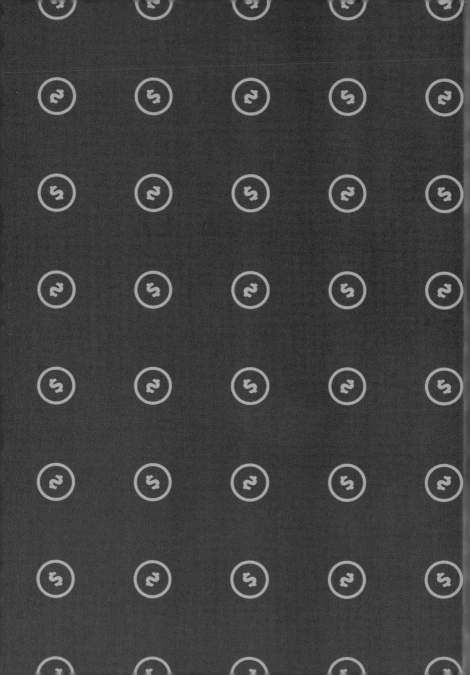